OCT 00

Kn

WOMEN'S PRO BASKETBALL TODAY

THE HISTORY OF THE DETROIT

SHOCK

AARON FRISCH

Published by Creative Education
123 South Broad Street, Mankato, Minnesota 56001
Creative Education is an imprint of The Creative Company

Design by Stephanie Blumenthal
Cover design by Kathy Petelinsek
Production design by Andy Rustad

Photos by: NBA Photos

Library of Congress Cataloging-in-Publication Data

Frisch, Aaron, 1975-
The History of the Detroit Shock / by Aaron Frisch
p. cm. — (Women's Pro Basketball Today)
Summary: Describes the history of the Detroit Shock professional women's basketball team
and profiles some of their leading players.
ISBN 1-58341-010-4

1. Detroit Shock (basketball team)—Juvenile literature. 2. Basketball for women—United States—
Juvenile literature. [1. Detroit Shock (Basketball team).
2. Women's basketball players. 3. Basketball players.] I. Title. II. Series.

GV885.52.D49F75   1999
796.323'64'0977434—dc21   99-18893

First Edition

2 4 6 8 9 7 5 3 1

As thousands of fans stream into the arena, a shockwave of anticipation rumbles through the Palace of Auburn Hills. When the Detroit Shock take the floor, wary opponents brace themselves for a high-voltage assault. Whether lighting it up from the perimeter, slashing to the hoop, or banging in the post, Detroit's young but hard-nosed squad brings heavy firepower to the hardwood every night. With a roster of budding stars that includes an All-WNBA leader, a Rookie of the Year runner-up, and one of the game's deadliest shooters—all directed by a basketball legend turned coach—the Shock have immediately become a formidable contender for the league crown.

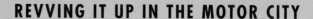 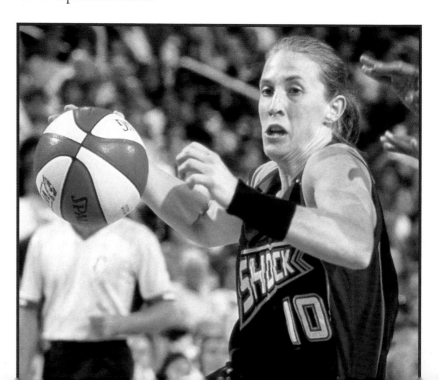

REVVING IT UP IN THE MOTOR CITY

Women's basketball was born in 1892 when Senda Berenson Abbott, a gym teacher at Smith College, introduced the game to her female students. But it wasn't until 105 years later that the women's game truly arrived. It was then that the Women's National Basketball Association was formed, giving female players a league of their own supported by nation-wide marketing, mass merchandise sales, and prime-time television broadcasting.

The WNBA's inaugural season was a rousing success that exceeded the expectations of even the most optimistic league supporters. Although teams were expected to play in front of modest crowds of 4,000, spectator numbers league-wide averaged more than 9,000 per game. All told, more than one million basketball fans came out to show support for the WNBA's eight fledgling teams over the course of the league's three-month season.

Not long after the WNBA's Most Valuable Player, Cynthia Cooper, led her Houston Comets to the first league crown in late August 1997, league president Val Ackerman and other WNBA officials began looking in earnest for two cities to be awarded new franchises. On October 1, the league announced Washington, D.C., and Detroit, Michigan, as recommended host cities for the two 1998 expansion teams.

DEANGELA MINTER (ABOVE); RHONDA BLADES OFFERED PLAYOFF EXPERIENCE (BELOW).

FORMER GLOBETROTTER LYNETTE WOODARD

Detroit, which had been home to the two-time world-champion Pistons of the National Basketball Association since 1957, embraced the idea from the start. A press conference soon followed the announcement, and Pistons All-Star forward Grant Hill, Pistons president Tom Wilson, and WNBA star Tina Thompson were present to show their enthusiasm. "I've followed and supported these [WNBA] athletes all season," Hill said. "I got an opportunity to watch a lot of WNBA games on television. Now I'm excited—I get to see them live and in person here in Detroit."

The Michigan metropolis' fans showed their excitement by ordering thousands of season tickets for their potential team. On November 11, after both cities reached their ticket-sales goals and fulfilled league marketing requirements, the WNBA made it official that Detroit and Washington would join the ranks of the young league in 1998. Both squads would be assigned to the Eastern Conference, with the Houston Comets moving over to the Western Conference.

Ackerman was pleased to add Detroit to the new league. "We like the idea of having another team in the Midwest," she said. "Everything about the city and the way the [Pistons] team has been run on the NBA side . . . is a formula for women's basketball to be successful in Detroit."

Two months later, Detroit's team found its identity when Tom Wilson, who would be president of the city's WNBA team as well, unveiled its name: the Shock. "It's electric—short and simple, yet powerful and memorable," Wilson explained. "Also, the name maintains our

organization's automotive connection, which was important as we began developing an identity for our new team."

The team's logo, revealed at the same time, is made up of the team's name and the league's ball surrounded by bright yellow lightning bolts and shockwaves. In keeping with the league's attempts to link its teams to their NBA counterparts in the same city, the Shock's colors are the same as those of the Pistons: black, teal, red, yellow, and metallic silver.

The Palace of Auburn Hills—a 20,000-seat arena that is home to the Pistons—would also be the home floor of the Shock. With pumped-up fans, an identity, and a home, the Shock was already resonating through Detroit four months before the season. "Our fans can begin getting excited about feeling the 'Shock Treatment' this summer," Wilson said.

LIEBERMAN-CLINE THROWS THE SWITCH

On January 12, 1998, the same day that Detroit basketball fans learned their new team's name, Tom Wilson introduced the Shock's first general manager and head coach. For both roles, he chose one of the most accomplished women's basketball players of all time: Nancy Lieberman-Cline.

Lieberman-Cline, who had come out of basketball retirement in 1997 to play for the Phoenix Mercury at the age of 38,

POST PLAYER TAJAMA ABRAHAM (ABOVE); HEAD COACH NANCY LIEBERMAN-CLINE (BELOW)

CENTER TAJAMA ABRAHAM

came to Detroit with one of the most illustrious careers in the history of the game. "Because she is one of the most well-known women to ever play the game," Wilson said, "she brings us instant name recognition and credibility [and is] someone we believed could build a winner from the ground up."

Lieberman (who added Cline to her last name after marrying former Continental Basketball Association player Tim Cline) was already one of America's best female players at the tender age of 15, when she held a spot on the United States National Team. At 18, Lieberman became the youngest player in basketball history to win an Olympic medal when she claimed silver as a member of the U.S. team. In a remarkable college career at Old Dominion, she led the Lady Monarchs to two straight national championships, was named an All-American three times, and won the Broderick Award as the nation's best female player as a senior.

As Old Dominion officials were still penning Lieberman's name all over the school's record books, the young standout was drafted as the top pick by the Dallas Diamonds of the Women's Professional Basketball League. Unfortunately, the WPBL and several other women's pro leagues within the next few years were forced to fold by a lack of fan support.

With the instability of women's basketball leagues, Lieberman soon looked into other opportunities. In 1981, she began a three-year stint as tennis star Martina Navratilova's personal trainer. After working in

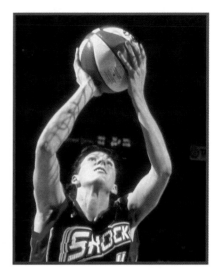

AUSTRALIAN

RACHAEL SPORN (ABOVE);

MOLLY TIDEBACK

(BELOW)

11

NAME: Nancy Lieberman-Cline

BORN: July 1, 1958

POSITION: Head Coach/General Manager

YEARS COACHED: 1998-present

RECORD: 17-13

As a collegiate player, Lieberman-Cline was a three-time All-American and two-time Wade Trophy winner for Old Dominion. She went on to play in four different professional basketball leagues and was named to the Naismith Memorial Basketball Hall of Fame in 1996. Lieberman-Cline played for the Western Conference Champion Phoenix Mercury in 1997 before taking on the challenge of piloting the expansion Shock the following season. The basketball legend headed every aspect of Detroit's creation, including decisions about personnel, drafting, player allocations, and team policies. Her first season results were impressive: a 17-13 record, a six-game winning streak, and a late run for a final playoff spot.

NAME: Sandy Brondello

BORN: August 20, 1968 (Mackay QLD., Australia)

POSITION: Guard

HEIGHT: 5-foot-7

COLLEGE: University of Western Sydney '90

Brondello was playing professionally in Germany when Detroit selected her in the fourth round of the '98 draft. Valued for her pure outside shooting and 10 years of professional experience, she surprised many by finishing ninth in league scoring with a 14.2 average. She tallied 98 assists and 38 steals on the season. First-season highlights included a personal-high 24 points against L.A. on August 19 and an eight-assist performance against Phoenix.

STATISTICS: 426 career points

Year	Average	Total Points	Avg. Assists
1998	14.2	426	3.3

sports broadcasting for several years, Lieberman joined the Springfield Fame (a United States Basketball Association team), becoming the first woman to ever play in a men's pro league.

In 1996, Lieberman-Cline became one of only 15 women to be inducted into the Naismith Memorial Basketball Hall of Fame. This honor was soon followed by the announcement that she would be one of the first inductees into the new Women's Basketball Hall of Fame in Knoxville, Tennessee.

Shock rookie guard Korie Hlede (pronounced Huh-LAY-day) knows first-hand that the competitive fire still burns in the savvy Hall-of-Famer. "I think [Lieberman-Cline is] demanding," Hlede said. "She was a great player, and, naturally, she doesn't want to lower her standards with us."

As Detroit's first head coach, Lieberman-Cline would be responsible for guiding the young Shock on the floor. But as general manager, she would also make all coaching staff and player decisions and be in charge of building the team roster. With the team's first training camp just three months away, Lieberman began assembling the Shock.

CINDY BROWN HAS A WARRIOR'S MENTALITY

A VETERAN FOUNDATION

For any expansion team, inexperience is always a major hurdle, and Lieberman-Cline knew that her young squad would need some seasoned guidance on the floor. Fortunately, this veteran foundation was soon established with the arrival of forward Cindy Brown and guard Lynette Woodard—one player at the top of her game and another drawing her amazing career to a close.

Cindy Brown became one of the first members of the Shock when she and center Razija Mujanovic were assigned to Detroit through the WNBA's Marquee Player Allocation program, a system designed to spread talent as evenly as possible throughout the league. Coach Lieberman-Cline was thrilled with Brown's arrival. "Cindy is one of the great competitors of women's basketball," she said. "She has a warrior's mentality. You might not know her at first, but when it's all said and done, she will be one of the top players in the WNBA."

As a collegiate star at Long Beach State, Brown once scored 60 points in a single game—an NCAA Division I record that still stands. Although a rookie in the WNBA, the 6-foot-2 and 183-pound forward came to Detroit following an 11-year professional career that included seasons in Seattle, Israel, Italy, and Japan. Brown can speak five languages, compliments of her extensive world travels.

CENTER TAJAMA
ABRAHAM (ABOVE);
FORWARD GERGANA
BRANZOVA (BELOW)

The versatile Brown was joined by one of women's basketball's active legends when the Shock acquired Lynette Woodard from the Cleveland Rockers on February 18. Woodard, who turned 39 midway through the 1998 season, was the oldest player to don a WNBA jersey, but the Shock coaching staff knew that the ageless wonder still had a lot to offer. "Lynette is a consummate professional," Lieberman-Cline said. "She's a great scorer, rebounder, and defensive player. . . . Lynette is a class act. She will be one of the leaders of this team on and off the court."

Woodard's storied basketball career began with her childhood dream of playing for the Harlem Globetrotters. "I talked about it from the time I was seven or eight years old," she recalled. The 6-foot guard put herself on the path to greatness at the University of Kansas, where the four-time All-American racked up 3,649 points, the most ever by a female collegiate player and second in major college basketball only to the legendary "Pistol" Pete Maravich.

After playing professionally overseas for a few years, Woodard realized her lifelong dream when she became the first female member of the Harlem Globetrotters in 1985. After spending three years with the traveling roundball

CO-CAPTAIN LYNETTE

WOODARD (ABOVE);

RHONDA BLADES

(BELOW)

show, she played three more seasons in Japan before retiring to become a stockbroker. Her love for the game, however, drew Woodard out of retirement in 1997, when she joined the Rockers.

Thanks to her change of heart, basketball fans around the league were given the opportunity to see one of the all-time greats grace the court. "Whenever she does decide to hang it up," said Mel Greenburg, member of the Hall of Fame nomination committee, "she'll get in [to the Hall of Fame] on the first ballot."

AN INTERNATIONAL CURRENT

In addition to Brown and Woodard, Lieberman-Cline found more good fortune when the league assigned Yugoslavia native Razija Mujanovic to Detroit. At 6-foot-8, the center brought exceptional size to the Shock, but she also brought 11 seasons of pro experience.

Throughout her career in Brazil, Spain, and Italy, the towering Mujanovic averaged nearly 20 points and 10 rebounds per game. Her consistently outstanding play earned her European Most Valuable Player honors four straight seasons between 1991 and 1995. "Razija will give us a legitimate chance to score every time on the block," Lieberman-Cline said. Mujanovic would be only the first of a stream of basketball talents that converged on Detroit from all parts of the world.

With the fourth pick overall in the 1998 WNBA draft, the Shock took Korie Hlede, an explosive guard just out of college. Hlede, a native of Croatia, rewrote the Duquesne University record books, shattering countless records, including points-per-game average with 24.1. "Korie is a tremendous scorer," Coach Lieberman-Cline said of the two-time Atlantic 10 Player of the Year. "She excels in a number of areas, distributes the basketball well, and can play defense."

Detroit solidified a potent backcourt by drafting Australian Sandy Brondello in the fourth round. Brondello, a 5-foot-7 guard, had played for the Australian National Team for seven years. Detroit fans were hoping that Brondello would give the Shock the firepower that had earned her two foreign-league MVP awards.

The Shock's head coach considered Rachael Sporn, another Australia native, to be one of Detroit's best catches. "Rachael is the type of player anyone would want on a basketball team," Lieberman-Cline said. "She has a load of talent, can run the floor, and has a nice medium-range jump shot." The 6-foot-1 jack-of-all-trades joined the WNBA after helping Australia win two world championships.

Carla Porter, the third Australian on the team, made the Shock roster through her impressive performance at the team's training camp tryouts. The 6-foot-1 forward, who was only 22 years old going into the 1998 season, had been part of Australia's National Team since she was 17.

Guard Rhonda Blades, a U.S. product who played for the WNBA's New York Liberty in 1997, was drafted to bring some

6-FOOT-2

REBOUNDING FORCE

CINDY BROWN

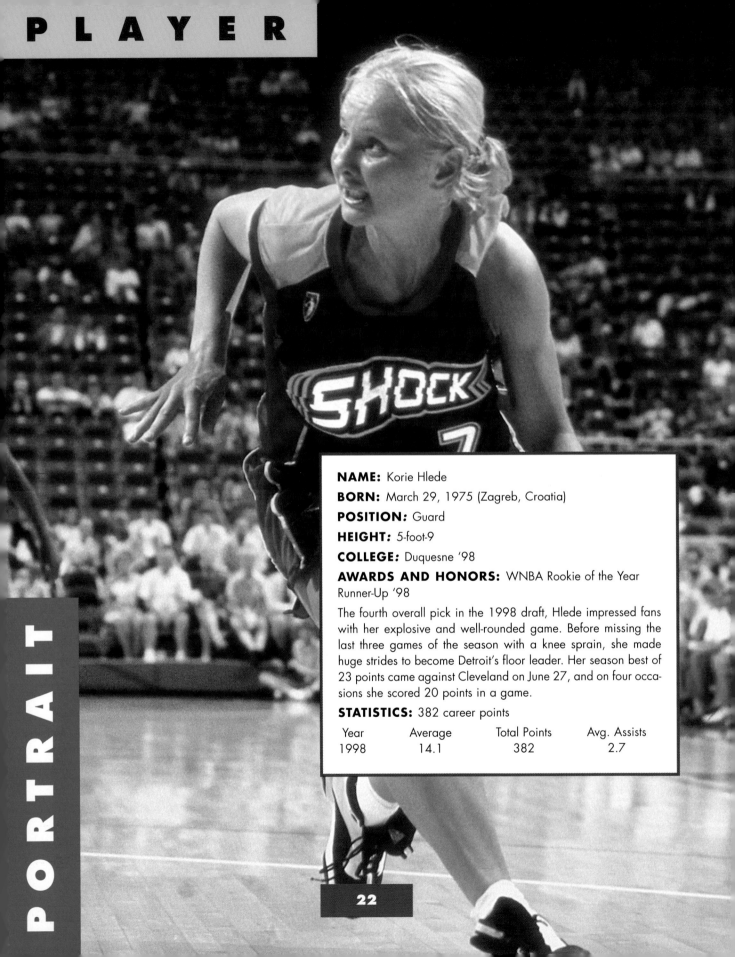

NAME: Korie Hlede

BORN: March 29, 1975 (Zagreb, Croatia)

POSITION: Guard

HEIGHT: 5-foot-9

COLLEGE: Duquesne '98

AWARDS AND HONORS: WNBA Rookie of the Year Runner-Up '98

The fourth overall pick in the 1998 draft, Hlede impressed fans with her explosive and well-rounded game. Before missing the last three games of the season with a knee sprain, she made huge strides to become Detroit's floor leader. Her season best of 23 points came against Cleveland on June 27, and on four occasions she scored 20 points in a game.

STATISTICS: 382 career points

Year	Average	Total Points	Avg. Assists
1998	14.1	382	2.7

NAME: Cindy Brown

BORN: March 16, 1965 (Portland, Ore.)

POSITION: Forward

HEIGHT: 6-foot-2

COLLEGE: Long Beach State '87

AWARDS AND HONORS: 1998 All-WNBA Second Team, Player of the Week 7-5-98

Assigned to the Shock through the WNBA Marquee Player Allocation program, Brown proved herself one of the most consistent performers in the league. Her 10 rebounds per game was .2 behind league leader Lisa Leslie. On August 10, the competitive forward nabbed a league-record 21 rebounds and added 10 points and four assists in a win over Utah.

STATISTICS: 354 career points

Year	Average	Total Points	Avg. Rebounds
1998	11.8	354	10.0

PORTRAIT

much-needed leadership and toughness to the Shock with her gritty and unselfish play. Blades, a 5-foot-7 guard that her coach calls "one of the most physical players anyone will play with in the league," was soon named team co-captain, along with Lynette Woodard.

Rounding out the Shock's first roster were Gergana Branzova, a 6-foot-4 forward from Bulgaria; Lithuanian guard Aneta "Angel" Kausaite; and 6-foot-2 American center Tajama Abraham. With its ethnically-mixed corps of talent in place, the Detroit Shock were ready for the WNBA.

BUILDING A CHARGE

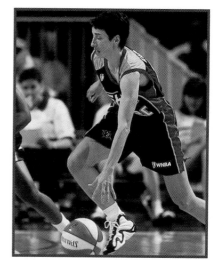

On June 13, 1998, after a month-long training camp, the Shock welcomed the Charlotte Sting to the Palace of Auburn Hills for the first WNBA game in Detroit history. A raucous crowd of 15,574 looked on as the Shock jumped out to a 10–2 lead four minutes into the game. But a furious 25–10 run put Charlotte up 39–30 at halftime, and the Sting hung on for a 78–69 win.

Despite the loss, the Shock showed clear signs of a promising future. Mujanovic dominated the paint, scoring 22 points and pulling down 13 boards, and Porter netted 13 points in a physical game. "We're very proud of our first game," Lieberman-Cline said afterward. "We're going to be a very good team."

Detroit would need to stay optimistic, as its first loss was followed by three more. Although all four games were tight, a lingering lack of familiarity between players left the Shock a little short in each contest. "We didn't get blown out," emerging star Korie Hlede said. "We had a lead in every game. We just didn't know how to really finish the game."

History was finally made on June 21, when the Shock traveled to play their sister expansion team, the Washington Mystics. Behind Hlede's 20-point performance, Detroit burst out to a 30–11 lead and never looked back, cruising to a 70–57 win. Cindy Brown, who added 11 points and continued her strong work on the boards,

explained the difference in the Shock's first-ever victory. "I think the turnaround was that we were tired of losing," she said simply. "It wasn't that other teams beat us [before]—we beat ourselves."

6-FOOT GUARD ANETA

KAUSAITE (ABOVE);

DEFENSIVE FORCE

BETSY HARRIS (BELOW)

25

Building on the confidence of its first win, Detroit went on a tear, winning a league-best six games in a row. Wins over Sacramento, Cleveland, Charlotte, and New York served notice to the league that the Shock were a force to be reckoned with. Detroit concluded its impressive streak with a dramatic 82–65 win over the New York Liberty at the Palace on July 1—Coach Lieberman-Cline's 40th birthday.

With the game knotted up at 62–62 with only two and a half minutes remaining, Brown scored to spark a 9–0 Shock run. Rookie phenom Hlede then took over, shredding New York for 11 of her 18 points in the final 84 seconds. Hlede, who was playing with a broken nose, sank nine straight free throws down the stretch to bury the stunned Liberty and cap an incredible 20–3 run. "Wow, what a birthday," a jubilant Lieberman-Cline said after the game. "I don't think I can remember a more fun day in my life." Brown helped make sure that her coach's big day was a memorable one by ripping up the Liberty with 22 points and 10 boards.

Unfortunately for Motor City fans, the Liberty exacted some revenge when the Shock came to town five nights later, squeaking past Detroit 59–56 and sending the Shock into another four-game losing skid. Although the upstart expansion team rolled into the season's mid-point at 7–8, teams around the league knew that a high-powered foe was rising in Detroit.

CINDY BROWN (ABOVE)

WAS NAMED TO THE

ALL-WNBA SECOND TEAM;

TARA WILLIAMS (RIGHT)

INCREASED VOLTAGE

After enduring their second tough losing streak, the Shock began to roll, winning two games for every loss in the second half of the season. The driving force behind Detroit's surprising charge was the high-octane scoring of Hlede and Brondello. Hlede, the team's 23-year-old floor general, carved up opposing defenses with 14.1 points a game, while Brondello added 14.2 points per contest with her deadly outside shooting. The Shock's greatest power, however, came from Cindy Brown, who dominated the glass with an average of 10 rebounds per night. "Cindy Brown is turning it on to a different level," Lieberman-Cline said.

With only four games remaining, the Shock—who, amazingly, found themselves in the hunt for a playoff spot—traveled to the ARCO Arena in Sacramento. Although the Shock took down the Monarchs 50–41 behind Brondello's 15-point showing, Detroit suffered a major blow when Hlede went down with a knee sprain. The loss of their explosive shooting guard proved costly three nights later, when the Shock fell to the powerful Phoenix Mercury.

Although Detroit finished the season strong, winning four of its last five games, it would finish just out of the playoff picture.

Hlede's injury left the Shock without a major weapon, but her absence quickly brought out the best in some of her teammates. Mujanovic, in particular, took her game to a new level, posting 15 points and six boards per game in Detroit's last three contests, including a team

YOUNG PHENOM

KORIE HLEDE (ABOVE);

AUSTRALIAN CARLA

PORTER (BELOW)

29

season-high 25 points against Los Angeles on August 16. "After three games," Lieberman-Cline joked, "I went into the locker room and looked at her and said, 'Who are you? Where's Razija?'"

Detroit finished its astonishing first season by dashing the playoff hopes of the New York Liberty with an 82–68 win in front of more than 16,000 fans at the Palace. With only four minutes remaining in the hard-fought game, Mujanovic sank a baseline hook shot, was fouled, and completed the three-point play to trigger an 11–2 Shock spurt.

The Shock converted 17 Liberty turnovers into 22 points and hit their last 19 free throws, finishing the game 25 of 27 from the charity stripe. Brondello concluded her outstanding season by scorching the Liberty for 24 points, and the ageless Woodard added a season-best 18 points and nine rebounds to help Detroit finish its inaugural season with 11 home wins and a 17–13 record.

BUILDING TOWARD GREATNESS

As the Detroit Shock closed the books on their extraordinary first season, Coach Lieberman-Cline had plenty of reasons to be optimistic about the franchise's future. Three of the biggest reasons were Brown, Brondello, and Hlede.

"Cindy Brown's consistency was unparalleled," the coach said. A 45-member media voting panel agreed by naming Brown to the All-WNBA Second Team. True to Lieberman-Cline's preseason prediction, Brown established herself as one of the WNBA's top stars. Over the course of the 30-game season, the forward averaged 11.8 points per game, and her 10 boards-per-game average was just .2 behind that of league rebounding champion Lisa Leslie of the Los Angeles Sparks

GUARD RHONDA BLADES

One of the Shock's most pleasant surprises was the solid play of Brondello, who dished out more than three assists per game in addition to her 14-point scoring average. Brondello, who made an incredible 96 of 104 free throws during the season, was awarded $12,500 as the league's best shooter from the foul line. "I've never won anything before playing basketball," the excited guard said. "And I'm one of the poorest players in the league."

But the main force behind the 1998 season—and, Lieberman-Cline hopes, the seasons ahead—was Korie Hlede, runner-up to the Charlotte Sting's Tracy Reid as the WNBA's Rookie of the Year. Her 39-percent three-point shooting, 5.2 boards per game, and 14-plus points per game make her a rising young talent who already plays like a veteran. "Korie Hlede is going to be a star in this league," her coach said. "We thought we were getting a good player, and she ended up being great for us."

Carla Porter, the second-youngest team member, helped Mujanovic in the frontcourt with 8.2 points per game, and the Shock received solid bench support. Reserves Sporn, Woodard, and Blades each gave Detroit between 11 and 18 minutes of quality play per game and consistently combined for double-digit bench scoring. "You expect your veterans to come in and play at a high level," Lieberman-Cline said, ". . . [but] our younger players gave more than we expected."

Although the Shock coach indicated that she would look for more athletic talent in future drafts to help Brown at the forward position, Lieberman-Cline and Detroit fans believe that they already have the nucleus of a winner. With an explosively talented mix of youth and experience guided by one of women's basketball legends, Detroit appears destined to stun the WNBA.